T0078405

ENJOY THE JOURNEY

Fourteen-Day Devotional

DENISE TAPIA

WESTBOW
PRESS®
A DIVISION OF THOMAS NELSON
& ZONDERVAN

WestBow Press books may be ordered through booksellers or by contacting:

WestBow Press
A Division of Thomas Nelson & Zondervan
1663 Liberty Drive
Bloomington, IN 47403
www.westbowpress.com
844-714-3454

ISBN: 978-1-6642-1872-7 (sc)
ISBN: 978-1-6642-1874-1 (hc)
ISBN: 978-1-6642-1873-4 (e)

Library of Congress Control Number: 2021900271

Print information available on the last page.

WestBow Press rev. date: 01/12/2020

This book is dedicated to you, the reader. May this book help you on whatever journey you're walking through. I hope you take the time to really dig deep in your journey to enjoy it. Don't be in a rush to get to your destination.

Contents

Acknowledgments

Special thanks to my pastors, Bobby and Ruby Magallanez. Thank you for pouring into me and believing in my God dreams. Thank you for equipping me for a moment such as this, and for pushing me to be more like Christ each and every day. The wisdom you've given me is how I was able to write this book.

Thank you to my parents and sisters for supporting me and helping me grow into the person that I am. Without you guys, I literally couldn't be here doing the things I'm doing. You're appreciated more than you know.

Thank you to my best friend, Faith Soto. You've called out the gold in my life and have supported every wild dream I've had—like publishing a book—since the day we met. I couldn't have done this without the inspiration, wisdom, love, support, and friendship you've given me. Thank you for walking along my journey with me and helping me find the joy in every situation.

To my team at WestBow Press, thank you for all the hard work you've done and help you've given during this process. Thank you for taking me on and allowing me to fulfill my dreams of becoming an author. Special thanks to Janine David.

Finally, to my Ascension City Church family, thank you for all your love and support. Each of you has challenged me and pushed me to be more like Christ.

Introduction

You are in a good place! Right there where you're at in life, you are in a good place! For so many years, I would look at the journey with God I was on and complain about the walk. I would think about all the uncomfortable situations God was taking me through, all the stretching I was doing, and how long the journey was taking to complete.

Then I read a verse that completely changed the way I looked at my journey: "Rejoice in our confident hope. Be patient in trouble, and keep on praying" (Romans 12:12). "Rejoice in hope." "Be patient in trouble." "Keep praying." Those words replayed in my mind for days as I thought about what they actually mean. In that season I felt like God was almost challenging me to find the joy in what I was walking through, to be patient on my journey, and to surrender fully all doubts, worries, and fears I had to Him.

Friends, when I say this was life-changing, I mean this was life-changing! Once I was able to find the joy, my perspective switched. My journey felt less like wandering in the wilderness and more like walking hand in hand with God as He guided me. Ever since that moment, I've been able to find the joy in every journey, and I've been able to take in all the things that God wants to teach me along the way and be transformed.

I want to share with you just a few things God has shown me and the ways I've been able to find the joy on my journey. These are small reminders I've needed daily, perspective switches I've had to make, and actions I've needed to take to truly understand where God is asking me to go on my journey.

I hope you have your walking shoes, a pen, highlighters, a journal, your Bible, and whatever else you may need because we're about to start a journey together, my friends! As we start this journey, let's ask God to open our eyes, our hearts, and our minds to show us the joy in our current journeys no matter what they look like. Let's ask Him to fill us with His Spirit and to give us the discipline, strength, and courage to keep going on the path He wants us on.

I hope you're as excited as I am! Let's get moving!

The
Journey

I feel like so many of us want all that God has planned for us and want to go to the places He's destined for us to go. But not many of us actually want to go on the journey to get there, or on the journey to be the people we need to be before we can take our first actual steps toward our destinations. On the journey we get dirty, we get broken down, we get pruned, and we get cultivated. New things are planted, and we have to be patient for the growth. The journey doesn't always feel like a road trip with your best friends. Sometimes it feels like being lost in the wilderness all alone. But that's not the case. The journey, for me, is more beautiful than the view when I finally get to the destination that God wants me at.

This whole journey I've been on the past couple of months has felt like walking on a treadmill. I feel like there's no progress being made, but I know I've got miles built up. I can't see myself getting any closer to my final destination, but I've got the mileage to prove that I'm closer than when I started. Our walks with God are like that, though. Sometimes we feel like we aren't getting any closer to Him, to our purposes, to our identities, to the destination that He predestined for us. In reality, we're moving closer to it than we think.

In times like this I have to remind myself constantly that I'm closer than where I started, I'm better off than where I began, and change is happening to me along the way. Even when we don't see an immediate change in our lives or in our situations, we trust that God is moving and at work in our lives.

Imagine for a minute you're on a road trip, long hours being cramped in a car, and the road seems like it goes on forever because all you're doing is driving straight. If you're from Texas like me, all you see is empty land on either side of you; you can go fifteen miles without the scenery changing even the slightest bit. That's a little bit like what the journey with God is like.

Maybe nothing seems to be changing around you. Maybe you feel like you're on a treadmill, and you aren't getting anywhere. Or maybe you're walking and growing tired because you don't see the progress. But let me tell you, friend, you're in a good place! Enjoy the journey; you will learn more along the way than you will when you finally get to your destination.

I press on to reach the end of the race and receive the heavenly prize for which God, through Christ Jesus, is calling us.

—PHILIPPIANS 3:14

Therefore, since we are surrounded by such a huge crowd of witnesses to the life of faith, let us strip off every weight that slows us down, especially the sin that so easily trips us up. And let us run with endurance the race God has set before us.

—HEBREWS 12:1

ASK GOD:

What journey am I on? What do
you want to show me, Lord?

Growing Pains

I remember the growing pains I felt as I grew up. The pain for me was almost unbearable sometimes, and lots of tears were shed. As much as I wanted to be taller, the truth is that growing hurts! I remember wanting to grow so much until I was in the middle of growing. Then pain made me content with being small.

The same is true of our faith. In order to grow we have to go through some pain. There have to be times of trial, tribulation, tests, stretching, or whatever you want to call it. And more often than not, it doesn't feel good. While the pain of growth doesn't feel pleasant, there is so much to be joyful for in this process!

James chapter 1 starts off talking about growth, and I love the perspective this chapter gives about growing: "So let it grow, for when your endurance is fully developed you will be perfect and complete" (James 1:4). Can you imagine a life where you've grown all you could possibly grow, and there is nothing more you could possibly need? That's the life I want to be living!

So many of us want the destination and the perfect growth, but no one wants the pains of growing. No one wants the discomfort, the stretching of our muscles, our spirits, or our faith. The truth is that the growing process is going to be painful. Moments will be unbearable, and you won't be comfortable, but the promise at the end is going to be so worth it. The promise that one day our endurance will be fully developed. We will be perfect and complete. We will need nothing.

As our muscles need to go through pain to grow, so does our faith. But don't be discouraged, friend. This growing process and pain will be beyond worth it when we are living in the fullness of who God created us to be. I believe that this pain will only last a little while, and the prize of being/fulfilling all God has purposed for you will last a lifetime. So let's grow, my friend!

For you know that when your faith is tested your endurance has a chance to grow. So let it grow, for when your endurance is fully developed, you will be perfect and complete, needing nothing.

—James 1:34

ASK GOD:

What area of my life needs
growth? How do I begin?

Unqualified

In today's world of comparison, it's easy to feel like you don't measure up. It's easy to think that there will always be someone better than you, someone more talented, someone with more experience, or someone with better qualifications. Whether you compare yourself to a friend, a coworker, or a sibling, it's easy to feel like you just aren't the right person for the job.

If I'm being honest, I know this feeling all too well. Even as I write this, right now my mind is saying, *Denise, who are you to be doing this? You don't have an English degree, you don't have a degree in theology, and you have absolutely zero experience in this!* The truth is that all those thoughts are correct. I have no experience in writing professionally. But what I do have is something that surpasses all worldly "qualifications." What I do have is a God who called me, who chose me, and a God who is sending me.

The amazing thing is the God who is doing all those things for me is doing the same things for you! God has a tendency to choose people society would label as "unqualified." If you look at the passage where the verse below comes from, God is telling Gideon he is about to lead an army into battle. Gideon isn't the guy you would choose to lead an army though. In fact, I would bet he's the last person you would've picked. Yet God chose him!

The beautiful thing is God didn't make him go through a training camp. God said, "Go with the strength you have." In whatever shape you are in, whatever season you are in, whatever knowledge you have, go with that. Whatever you have is more than enough for God to use. He doesn't need perfection; He needs a willing heart.

What is God asking you to do? Where is He calling you to go? Take time to really press in, and ask God what He wants from you. Write down your answers and then ask for strength, confidence, boldness, and to help you truly believe that you are who God wants to use.

Then the Lord turned to him and said, "Go with the strength you have, and rescue Israel from the Midianites. I am sending you!"

—JUDGES 6:14

ASK GOD:

What are You asking me to do?
How do I take the first step?

Denise Tapia

Heart
Hurts

How many of us have gone through heartbreak/heartache? Maybe it's because of a breakup, death of a loved one, depression, extreme trauma; the list goes on. When our hearts feel those pains, we cope in different ways. We might eat a tub of ice cream, binge watch Netflix, cry ourselves to sleep, or lose our appetites, just to name a few. Some of us express that pain in different ways—writing (totally me!), making music, painting/drawing, creating sculptures, and so on. While all these things are okay to do—some in moderation—there is one thing we often don't do first that we should do.

When we feel our hearts hurt, the first thing we should turn to is God. Many of us go first to the worldly remedies and coping mechanisms instead of taking those hurts straight to the Source to heal every wound and hurt our hearts feel. God is the One, and only one, who can heal every bit of hurt that our hearts feel. God is the One who mends and transforms our hearts and the One who can give us completely new hearts that line up with His.

During those moments of complete heartache, there is one thing that our hearts are longing to do—speak with the Lord! When our hearts hurt, it's their way of telling us they need to plug into the Creator to heal. They need to go to the ultimate heart surgeon to mend the pain. God wants all our hearts, and that includes when our hearts are completely and totally broken/shattered. There is nothing our hearts could go through that is too much for God!

The amazing thing is that once we take our heartaches to God, He instantly begins to heal them. Once we lay all our messes at the feet of Jesus, there is a peace and a comfort that surpasses all understanding waiting for us. God loves you and wants every part of you to come to Him, not just the pretty, well-kept parts.

If your heart is in pain today, you're in a good place, my friend. There is a Father who loves you and is waiting for you to go lay it all down at His feet. He's waiting to have a conversation with you. Go and speak with Him. His ears are wide open for you!

My heart has heard you say, "Come and talk with me." And my heart responds, "Lord, I am coming."

—Psalm 27:1

The Lord is close to the brokenhearted; he rescues those whose spirits are crushed.

—Psalm 34:18

ASK GOD:

What hurts does my heart still need healing from? Heal my heart, Lord.

With Me

There is a big God who created us! A God who's omnipotent, omniscient, and omnipresent, which is the fancy way of saying that God is all-powerful, all-knowing, and is everywhere! We can go on and on about how powerful and mighty God is, so much so that we can get lost in how big He is, and we forget just how personal God actually is.

It's easy to lose God in our struggles, in the trenches, in the middle of our battles, in the middle of our daily lives. We forget that God is everywhere, including our messes. God knows everything, including the hurts and secrets we keep in our hearts and minds. And we forget that God is all-powerful, including powerful enough to see you through to the other side of your battles.

Imagine for a second that God is sitting right next to you where you're reading this. Imagine God already knows every thought you have right now about what you're reading. Imagine that God has already won the battle you're going through in life right now. Through God you have that same power to overcome. How personal did God just become to you?

In your current life situation, God is with you, God knows your thoughts, and God knows the battles you're facing. God isn't just a big man in the sky; He is your Father! And as your Father, He cares for you so deeply. He is right there in the trenches with you in every battle you face. In the darkest of your thoughts, the secrets you don't want anyone to know because they're ugly, God sees them and loves you through them.

God is everywhere, but God is everywhere *with you*. God knows everything, but God knows everything *about you*. God created everything, and God *created you.* God is so much more personal than you know, and He is with you every day of your life. Take the time today to look for God in your life. Take the time to see Him as you sit at work or go to the grocery store. As you question how God could love or use someone like you, knowing how your mind works. As you question why God made you the way that He did. Remember, friend, God is with you and for you!

O Lord, you have examined my heart and know everything about me.

—Psalm 139:1

You go before me and follow me. You place your hand of blessing on my head.

—Psalm 139:5

You made all the delicate, inner parts of my body and knit me together in my mother's womb. Thank you for making me so wonderfully complex! Your workmanship is marvelous—how well I know it.

—Psalm 139:14–15

ASK GOD:

Show me the places I've missed You
being in the rooms of my life.

Work of Art

We often find awe in the natural things in the world around us but look at ourselves in the mirror as ordinary at best. We look at nature—how things are naturally formed, how beautiful they are—and we are in amazement at these things. We could stare for hours at ocean waves crashing down. We could watch a sunrise and sunset over and over and never grow tired of it. We could explore a cave and see how over time these wonders were created. Many of us have done these things or others similar to appreciate the world around us. While it's always good to appreciate all that God has created, we never really do appreciate everything. The greatest work of art He has and will ever make is probably the least appreciated. I'm talking about you, His child!

It's not easy for us—especially women—to see ourselves as beautiful. There is always going to be something about ourselves that will keep us from thinking we are in any way, shape, or form in the same class of beauty as something like a sunset. When we look into the details of a sunset, it just gets more beautiful, but when we look into the details of us, we tend to find more flaws than we thought we had. It's no surprise that in today's society, body image, and looks are the biggest insecurities of both men and women. When we think of ourselves and then think of the sunset, we could wonder, *God, how could You make a sunset look better than me?* and get upset. But let me share with you what God revealed to me that completely rocked my world.

When God created everything, He called it "good." Not great, not amazing, not breathtaking, just "good." For you and I, though, God describes us with words like "masterpiece," "precious," "honored," and, "loved," because to our Creator/Father, we are the greatest things He could've ever created.

For we are God's masterpiece. He has created us anew in Christ Jesus, so we can do the good things he planned for us long ago.

—Ephesians 2:10

Others were given in exchange for you. I traded their lives for yours because you are precious to me. You are honored, and I love you.

—Isaiah 43:4

ASK GOD:

Help me see myself the way
You see me, Lord.

Hearing
Heart

If God came to you right now and said, "Whatever you ask Me for right now, it's yours!" what would be the one thing you asked for? Would it be good health? Protection over the people you loved? Fame, fortune, or a high follower count? Or would you dig a little deeper for something more spiritual and less materialistic? I would love to believe that I would pick something deep and spiritual, but if I'm being real, that probably wouldn't be the case. And I'm sure the same is true for many of you.

This opportunity was presented to Solomon, and do you know what he asked for? An understanding heart! Some people might wonder, *Out of anything in the world he could've asked for, that was really what he wanted? That's crazy!* Which is true. I can't imagine many of my friends or family members asking for an understanding heart. But the truth of the matter is an understanding heart is what we all should ask God for on a daily basis!

In the original Hebrew text, the word for understanding is *Shâma'* (shaw-mah): "to hear intelligently (often with impl. of attention, obedience, etc.) Diligently discern, give ear". 1. *The New Strong's Complete Dictionary of Bible Words*, s.v. shâma', accessed 1996.

When Solomon asked for an understanding heart, what he was really asking for was a hearing heart! A heart to hear what though? What could your heart possibly need to hear? In this instance, Solomon wanted a heart that would hear God, a heart that was guided by God, a heart that had the wisdom only God could give.

Can you imagine having that heart? Can you imagine going through everyday life and every time something didn't go the way you planned, or every time a problem occurred, maybe an argument broke out, and so on, you had the heart to listen to God during those moments? You could take in everything that was happening around you and listen to God to hear and discern what it was that you needed to do or say. You see, shâma' isn't just about listening; it's about obedience! It's one thing to hear what God is telling you to say or do, but it's another thing to actually obey those things! My friend, God doesn't want you to just hear His words when He speaks to you. He wants you to obey. He wants you to be truly surrendered and guided by Him.

Solomon is known for his wisdom, and that wisdom he didn't get on his own. Solomon asked for a hearing heart, for wisdom, that could only come from God. You and I could have the same wisdom! You and I could have the same heart that is guided by God, that is listening to hear God's voice in every situation, ready to obey what He tells us. My prayer for you is that you desire a hearing heart. That you live in wisdom to do and say all that God is speaking to you, and you are actively listening to what God is speaking to your heart.

Give me an understanding heart so that
I can govern your people well and know
the difference between right and wrong.
For who by himself is able to govern this
great people of yours?

—1 KINGS 3:9

ASK GOD:

Tune my heart to listen to and
obey Your Word, Lord.

What Did I Come Here for Again?

Have you ever had that moment when you entered a room, paused, and asked yourself, *What did I come in here for again?* Then you had to stand there for a good while, maybe longer than you'd like to admit, to remember. Or maybe you don't remember and leave frustrated because you forgot. I'm totally guilty of those moments, and when I forget, I get so upset with myself! And I know I'm not the only one!

So many times I think we're all guilty of these questions when it comes to our purposes: "God, why am I on earth again?" "God, what's my purpose again?" "God, what did I come here for?" I'll be the first to admit, I ask them way too often. It's almost like we forget purpose, and we totally forget what we're doing.

When this happens and we can't remember, or maybe God doesn't answer this question as fast as we want, we start to get frustrated. We get frustrated with ourselves and with God. We get upset and start to feel like maybe we don't even have a purpose, and that's such a dangerous place to be! But let me pop those thought bubbles right now for you, friend, God created you with a purpose. You're on this earth for a reason, and God has big plans for you!

When it comes to our purposes, many of us want this big blueprint rolled out in front of us, telling us exactly what we're supposed to do and how we're supposed to accomplish it. And more times than not, that's not the way God is going to reveal our purposes to us. What I've come to learn is that God will tell me *why* I'm on this earth, but when it comes to the *how* I'm supposed to live out the why, God allows me to search Him and figure that out.

For all humanity the why we are on this earth is the same, to be a reflection of God and to love people the way God loves us. The answer to the question, "What did I come here for again?" my friend, you came here to love people with all you have. You've been placed here on this earth to reflect God, to be the light, to show people who Jesus is, and to show people to a God who loves them deeply.

Now that you know why you're on this earth, what are you gonna do next? How are you going to show the people in your world the love of God? How are you going to live out the purpose that God has placed inside you? God has so many big plans for you, my friend, and while I can't tell you exactly what those plans are or how they're going to come about, I can tell you the place to start looking. Start searching in God's Word and in prayer with Him! Start by loving the people around you in life, and spread that love like wildfire. You came here to love like Jesus!

Jesus replied, "You must love the Lord your God with all your heart, all your soul, and all your mind." This is the first and greatest commandment. A second is equally important: "Love your neighbor as yourself." The entire law and all the demands of the prophets are based on these two commandments.

—MATTHEW 22:37–40

Therefore go and make disciples of all the nations, baptizing them in the name of the Father and the Son and the Holy Spirit. Teach these new disciples to obey all the commands I have given you. And be sure of this: I am with you always, even to the end of the age.

—MATTHEW 28:19–20

ASK GOD:

Remind me what you purposed me for.

Squad
Goals

Who do you surround yourself with? In your current life, where you are, what kind of people do you surround yourself with? Do you have friends who are exactly like you? Or maybe friends who are polar opposites, and that's why you get along so well? I think we've all—or most of us—have heard the saying, "Show me your five closest friends, and I'll tell you who you are." It wasn't until I became a young adult that I really understood what that saying actually meant.

God created us to be in community. God wants us to surround ourselves with people. Not just any people, but people who will help us grow and who will encourage us to be all that He created us to be. In my circle of friends, I have people who have pushed me to grow closer to Jesus and friends who have encouraged me and call out the gold in my life.

Denise Tapia

My past friendships haven't always been the same way, though, and I'm betting many of y'all can relate to that.

In Mark 2:1–12 you can read about a paralyzed man who was healed because his friends literally carried him to Jesus so he could be healed. Talk about squad goals! How many of your friends in your spheres right now would carry you to the feet of Jesus because you had no strength left to get there on your own? Better yet, how many of you would be that friend to carry someone to Jesus because your friends can't get there on their own?

Friends, as we go forward in life, let's strive to be the friend who helps lead others back to Jesus, as well as surrounding ourselves with these types of friends. As you go about your day, think about the friendships you have in life, and really ask God if they are hurting you or propelling you. God wants you to have a community in your corner on this journey you're on to help you fulfill the God dreams He's placed inside you. Let's surround ourselves with the right friends as we move forward on this journey!

Four men arrived carrying a paralyzed man on a mat. They couldn't bring him to Jesus because of the crowd, so they dug a hole through the roof above his head. Then they lowered the man on his mat right down in front of Jesus. Seeing their faith, Jesus said to the paralyzed man, "My child, your sins are forgiven."

—MARK 2:3–5

As iron sharpens iron, so a friend sharpens a friend.

—PROVERBS 27:17

ASK GOD:

Is my circle of friends propelling me to be more like You?

Fully Surrendering

Surrender is often looked at as such a weak concept. The world has made surrender a term reflecting giving up, of throwing in the towel. But in the terms of God, surrender is actually one of the most powerful moves to make. Fully surrendering to God means throwing your hands off the steering wheel and saying, "God, you drive cause I'm not sure which way to go!"

For a good part of my walk with God, I thought being fully surrendered was a one-time thing. I thought it meant that the one time I said, "God, you take control of every part of my life," was enough to cover me for all my days to come. But let me tell you, friends, I was wrong! Fully surrendering is something we actively have to do on this journey we're on. It's an everyday decision to give God control of your life, to allow His will, not ours, to be done.

Let's take a moment to close our eyes and imagine what life would look like if we fully surrendered to God every moment of our lives. Seriously, close your eyes and imagine for a moment! Did you see yourself bringing peace to arguments? Did you see God opening doors you didn't even know you could walk through? Did you see God using you to pray for people at grocery stores? Did you see yourself moving in ways you never dreamed of moving in? Friends, being fully surrendered to God is a day-by-day, moment-by-moment thing you have to do.

In the middle of a conversation that seems to be getting heated, surrender to God, and listen to what He tells you to say and do. When making a career choice, surrender it to God, and listen for which direction He's telling you to move. When an opportunity arises, surrender to God and ask if this is the right move to make, and be obedient to what that answer is.

As you go about your day, ask God how He wants you to surrender in every moment. Ask God if there's something big you need to do—end a friendship/relationship, have a hard conversation with a boss/coworker, step out of your comfort zone to help someone in need. Maybe it's something small, like being the peace in an argument, telling someone at the store that Jesus loves him or her, or paying for someone else's coffee. Whatever it may be, friends, surrender fully to God, and watch how He moves in you and through you! Remember, take it moment by moment. He is with you every step of the way.

Trust in the Lord with all your heart; do not depend on your own understanding. Seek his will in all you do, and he will show you which path to take.

—PROVERBS 3:5–6

Submit to God, and you will have peace; then things will go well for you.

—JOB 22:21

ASK GOD:

What do I need to surrender to You fully?

Even If

The biggest thing that has kept me from following God 100 percent is fear, fear of the ifs. You know, the fear of the things that haven't happened yet, but you think about them as though they were happening right before your eyes. I can't tell you how many times those made-up scenarios in my head have kept me from doing what God has called me to do. And there is always so much regret when I let those fears get to me.

Satan loves to scare us with those scenarios. He loves to just punk us out from serving and following God with everything we have by giving us the if situations to think about. "God, I'll follow You *if* it's easy." "God, I'll serve You *if* I don't have to work too hard." "God, I'll love You *if* it doesn't cost me anything." "God, I want to tell people about You, but what *if* people think I'm weird?" "God, I know You're calling me on a mission, but what *if* something happens to me there?" Do any of these sound familiar to you?

There are so many ifs we have with God, but could you imagine living life without any ifs when it comes to living for God? Or maybe just changing "if" to "even if," and instead saying, "God I'll love You *even if* it costs me everything." "God, I'll serve You *even if* I have to work harder than I ever have before in my life!" "God, I'll follow You *even if* it's the hardest thing I've ever done!" "I'm gonna tell the world about You *even if* I look like the biggest weirdo in the world!"

Despite all the ifs that the enemy might throw at us, God is still God! Believing and living for God without fear of the ifs is exactly what faith is. It's knowing whose you are and who is on your side and then deciding to follow no matter what.

Friends, today let's commit to following God despite the even ifs of life! Because despite what happens in our lives, God is still good, God is still in control, and God is still for you.

If we are thrown into the blazing furnace, the God whom we serve is able to save us. He will rescue us from your power, Your Majesty. But even if he doesn't, we want to make it clear to you, Your Majesty, that we will never serve your gods or worship the gold statue you have set up.

—DANIEL 3:17–18

ASK GOD:

What situation in my life right now is making me doubt? How can I have the strength to overcome the ifs?

Remind Me

Small reminders from people we love or our friends are always good to hear. For example, when someone tells you he or she appreciates you; loves you; that you're doing a good job; or that you're valued, loved, and believed in. Those are all great reminders to get because, let's be real, we forget those things! We get so caught up with life that we forget the little things that happen to us throughout the day.

The same thing happens with God. We sometimes forget all the ways God moves and shows up in our lives. I'm gonna be 100 percent transparent with you: I sometimes forget how God has shown up in my life. It's not that I forget who God is or what He can do, but I forget how good God has been to me and what He's done in my life. Sometimes I need the reminder that God is the same; what He's done in the past for me, He can do again.

It's so easy for us to remember things God has done in the Bible. But when it comes to recalling how God shows up for us personally, we have a hard time seeing God's hand or remembering what He did. But those reminders of how God has moved in our lives in the past strengthens our hopes for the future. Because God did it once, we can rest assured that He has the power to perform miracles again and again in our lives!

Just when all hope might be lost, ask God to remind you—remind you of His love, remind you of the times He's been right beside you, remind you of the ways He's moved in your life when you thought there was no hope, remind you of the battles He fought on your behalf. You'll be surprised by the things He'll show you.

Today let's ask God to do just that. Let's ask God to remind us. Right there where you're at, ask God, and as He begins to bring back these memories, write them down. Put them in a journal you can go back to every time you need that reminder. Then just thank God for His love, His goodness, and His mercy. It's time we're reminded of just how much God has done for us, friends.

But then I recall all you have done, O Lord; I remember your wonderful deeds of long ago. They are constantly in my thoughts. I cannot stop thinking about your mighty works.

—Psalm 77:11–12

ASK GOD:

Remind me where You've shown up in my life, remind me of Your love. Remind me of my first yes.

Run the Race

The most I've ever run without stopping once was six miles. That may not seem like much to my friends who are marathon runners, but this was huge for me! It took a lot of work, training, and pushing myself to the limits to get to this distance, and if I'm being real, this process was not fun. I wanted to quit so many times. I wanted to just stop running and walk my way home. But I had set a goal for myself, and I was determined to meet that goal.

Whether we like to run or not, we're all running a race. We're all running toward the prize of righteousness, toward the prize of being in heaven again with our Father, toward the prize to fulfill purpose. The race we're running isn't about speed though; it's not about how fast you can get to the end but how hard you push yourself to keep going. It's about how much you endure yet never cease to run. It's about running freely without thought of how hard other people are running around you. It's about running fiercely because you're determined to make it to the end. It's about running focused on God, the only One who will see you to the end!

Friends, this race is hard, this race is tiring, this race is painful. But this race has a far better prize than anything this world has to offer! Walking the race isn't an option anymore because we're running to win. You were made to run this race. Don't give up! Focus on the One who has placed you in the race, and turn to Him for help. You can do this!

Run fiercely, run freely, run focused on God! The race may be far from over, but the prize at the end is worth it, my friend. Don't settle for walking the race; run with everything you have. This is what you were made for!

Therefore, since we are surrounded by such a huge crowd of witnesses to the life of faith, let us strip off every weight that slows us down, especially the sin that so easily trips us up. And let us run with endurance the race God has set before us. We do this by keeping our eyes on Jesus, the champion who initiates and perfects our faith. Because of the joy awaiting him, he endured the cross, disregarding his shame. Now he is seated in the place of honor beside God's throne.

—HEBREWS 12:1-2

Don't you realize that in a race everyone runs, but only one person gets the prize? So run to win! All athletes are disciplined in their training. They do it to win a prize that will fade away, but we do it for an eternal prize. So I run with purpose in every step. I am not just shadow boxing.

—1 CORINTHIANS 9:24–26

ASK GOD:

What do I need to stop focusing on to better focus on You, Lord? What's tripping me up on my race?

In the Wild

There's a pretty popular television show called *Naked and Afraid* that made me realize just how comfortable my life is. The show takes one naked man and one naked woman and places them in the middle of the wilderness. Each has only one tool to help them survive for twenty-one days. They have to find food, water, shelter, and so on all on their own, with only themselves to rely on. More often than not, people quit before the twenty-one days are up because they can't do it. The challenge is definitely tough, and I'm surprised people are willing to even go through that.

Thinking about this show, I become so grateful for my comfortable living, a house, A/C, a refrigerator full of food, heater for the winter; I have it made! There isn't really anything I rely on because I have everything to keep me comfortable. Then it dawned on me that while I'm comfortable, I stop relying on

God. Why should I rely on God when I'm perfectly fine, when life is good, and there's no struggle? I pray, read my Word, and go to church, but there isn't a reliance on God to keep me alive.

But when seasons come that are uncomfortable, rough, and all around not fun to be in, boy do I panic, I complain, I whine, I groan, I mumble under my breath. Yet it takes me a while to turn to God for help. I look at those seasons and call them "wilderness seasons" because I'm uncomfortable the way I'd be in the wilderness, almost like a spiritual *Naked and Afraid*. Like the show, I have one tool, the only one I need to help me survive the wilderness. But I don't turn to my tool as quickly as I should, waiting until I'm about to give up.

That tool is God. The wilderness, though uncomfortable, allows me to learn how to rely on God completely. It allows me to grow in ways I can't when I'm comfortable. It allows me to find peace where I can't because of the noises in my life. And it allows me to find God in a deeper way.

I'm reminded of the time Jesus was tempted in the wilderness for forty days and forty nights. Yes, even Jesus had a wilderness season! He made it through because though He was in the wilderness hungry and uncomfortable, He relied on God. He had no other choice but to rely on God if He wanted to make it out. If we go back to the Old Testament, the Israelites had a very long wilderness season. God guided them through the wilderness for forty years! While in their wilderness season, they had to rely on God for literally everything—food, water, and guidance on which way to go.

Friends, while on this journey, you are going to enter some wilderness seasons. It's going to be uncomfortable, it might hurt a little, and it'll test you for sure. But it's only when we rely on God to lead us through that we'll make it out on the other side. On the other side of the wilderness for the Israelites was the Promised Land; on the other side of the wilderness for Jesus was ministry work to begin. Ask God today what's on the other side of your wilderness season and what lessons He wants you to learn, and put your full trust in Him.

The wilderness is just a season on the journey. Find joy in the journey by finding God in the wilderness. There are some things He wants to show you that can only be seen when you're fully reliant on Him. You're gonna come out of the wild strong, equipped, and ready for the next journey!

Then Jesus was led by the Spirit into the wilderness to be tempted there by the devil.

—MATTHEW 4:1

When Pharaoh finally let the people go, God did not lead them along the main road that runs through Philistine territory, even though that was the shortest route to the Promised Land. God said, "If the people are faced with a battle, they might change their minds and return to Egypt." So God led them in a roundabout way through the wilderness toward the Red Sea. Thus the Israelites left Egypt like an army ready for battle.

—EXODUS 13:17–18

ASK GOD:

What's on the other side of the wilderness for me? What are You preparing me to do, Lord?

Printed in the United States
By Bookmasters